CHANGE YOUR VOCABULARY

CHANGE YOUR VOCABULARY

TEN EASY RULES TO IMPROVE THE
QUALITY OF YOUR LIFE FOREVER.

WILLIAM MICHAEL BASTAS

AUSTIN

CONTENTS

PART I.
THE RULES

DEDICATED TO MY LATE WIFE

MICHELLE 1954-2006

PREFACE

My career as a photographer has afforded many varied assignments. Among them was the responsibility of photographing man's grandest celebration, The Wedding!

Other professions offer this type of experience over a lifetime, including hairstylist, bartender, and cab drivers to name a few. They become the chronicler of the human experience. During weddings, the photographer can see the best and worst of human relationships. I have observed families who exhibit the most love, whose children grow into excellent people having greater success overall, seem to share one thing in common.

They all have a deep-rooted faith. It doesn't matter the religion; be it Christianity, Islam, Judaism, or Buddhism or others, their faith plays a pivotal role in the family. The sum and substance of this book require faith in 'The Creator God.'

There can only be one God. Belief in The Higher Power is the only requirement to make these rules work for you.

INTRODUCTION

CHANGE YOUR VOCABULARY!

TEN EASY RULES TO IMPROVE THE QUALITY OF YOUR LIFE FOREVER.

This easy to read and understand the book will give you enough material to improve the quality of your life in every way.

'Change Your Vocabulary' means a simple rephrasing of life's conditions can be instrumental in turning them from something negative to something positive.

Everyone knows that a positive mental attitude (PMA) is an essential ingredient to happy and successful living. Many programs and books have been written on the subject by people like Dr. Maxwell Maltz, Dr. Norman Vincent Peale, Robert Collier, Dr. Wayne Dyer, and others. I encourage you to read some or all of them.

I believe these writers often don't go far enough to explain why PMA works. Just what are the reasons these programs, followed faithfully work for some people and not for others?

Let me clear the air on one thing. It doesn't matter which writer's philosophy you embrace as long as it works for you!

The problem arises when a program doesn't

work, because you don't understand how or why it works, and you give up.

I will share ten rules 'sound familiar,' simple rules, to a fuller understanding of how the power of your thoughts, deeds, and words will change your life forever!

The Rules:

Never give up!

Never worry about things over which you have no control.

Nothing happens by accident. Everything happens for your good.

Be careful of your wishes. Be mindful of what you say.

Listen to 'the teacher within.'

An idle mind is the 'devil's workshop.'

We are ruled by our weakness.

Surrender big problems to 'The Greater Power.'

Give yourself the same 'slack' that you give everyone else.

'Be nice to the people.'

These rules are in no particular order. Each one is as important as the next.

ABOUT THE AUTHOR

I was born in January of 1941 in Chicago, IL. The son of a Greek immigrant and an Indiana farm girl. We lived on the old West Side of the inner city. In many ways, life for me then was like a combination of 'Happy Days' TV show and the movie, 'Goodfellas' and from Broadway's, West Side Story! We never owned a car, a home, or had any money to spare. My dad was not well educated, nor was my mother. Dad was a peddler of fresh cut flowers to the florist trade throughout the city. During the winter months, my mother would have to take an occasional factory job to help the family make ends meet. In those days, the idea of being on government welfare was considered a disgrace.

The Second World War broke out later in 1941, and it hadn't been very long since the Great Depression.

When I was in grammar school, we must have moved three or four times. Living in buildings that were condemned, by Cook County, scheduled for demolition to make room for the large medical center of today. We lived in flats (apartments) with cheap rent, but we had to move often, which meant a few changes in schools, new friends, and new routines. This photo is of the old run-down county-owned apartment where we lived and the last place I lived in Chicago. Looking back, I suppose it was tough.

While still in 7th or 8th grade, I worked with my dad in the summers, bringing the flowers from the growers to the florists in the inner city. I cherished the work. Watching Dad argue with the florists over a nickel a dozen for the price of Gladiolas or Peonies was quite an education.

In my high school years, I worked in the neighborhood pizza place owned and run by two Sicilian immigrants, earning just a dollar an hour.

To this day, people tell me I make the best pizza around. I got 'street smart' working in that pizza joint! I learned from the good cops, the crooked cops, the parish priests, and the wheeler-dealers of the neighborhood. Yeah, it was tough! You learned to fight, literally, for what you had and fight to keep it, but I wouldn't trade that experience for any other in the world.

I managed to finish high school but thought getting out into the world to 'make a buck' was more important than college. A decision I came to wish I hadn't made. My first job was as a mailroom boy for Chicago Title and Trust. I loved the job because I got to meet everyone in the building as I made my rounds. The job paid $225.00 per month. Even in 1959, that just wouldn't cut it.

I quit that job to join the Teamsters Union to work in the trucking industry. Working on the docks tracing lost freight, starting at $175.00 per week. My dad told me it was a "big mistake." He may well have been right; however, the lure of $175.00 per week was just too strong

In 1960 I married young, we had kids young, and responsibilities beyond even the $175.00 per week job. That led me to a career in sales. A new baby and we were still living in that old apartment building. A man knocked on my door selling baby furniture. I loved the product and the concept of marketing to young parents-to-be. I didn't know then, but recruiting new salespeople was the lifeblood of his business. When I asked him for a job, he was more than willing to get me started, this was door-to-door, sales carrying samples to the prospect's home and I loved it. This job got me started in direct sales.

I was good at the job, and before long, I became his business partner. It was an exciting time! A new role that paid well and a new baby, and another on the way, we even bought our first house.

In a couple of years, I went to work, also as a direct outside salesman, for one of the largest carpet retailers in the Chicago area. That was quite an education for me. It was here, looking back, that the basis for this book was born. To make a long story short, that was the last job I ever had. From the age of twenty-three, I have been self-employed. Let me tell you keeping your head straight is critical when you are responsible for everything you get. Now, over fifty years later,

I want to share what I have learned with you in the hope that it will enrich your life as it has mine.

PART I

THE RULES

1

NEVER GIVE UP

Much of what you read in this book will help you to lead a more productive life. I am not saying that we can be in total control of 100% of the time. Life is about trial and error, making mistakes, then adjusting to a better path.

Life gives you two options. There is up or down, white or black, forward or backward. While there may appear to be shades of gray, but in the last analysis, there are only two decisions. Yes or no! You are free to choose your option.

The path you select will determine your success or failure.

I can best illustrate this concept with a very personal example.

The following example of 'Never Give Up!'

There was a turbulent time in the early '70s, and I was going through many changes. I have always had a fondness for luxury cars and have owned many; I wish I still had, like a '62 Pontiac Bonneville, '64 Cadillac Convertible and a '72 Lincoln Continental.

This story is about the beautiful 1972 Lincoln

Continental, black, sleek, elegant, and proud. When I bought that car, I thought I had really '*made it.*'

I drove the car around Dallas, Texas, as if I was sitting on top of the world. I had riding horses, a great job, and family. It looked like I was on the way to the top.

One thing sure in life is change. *Change* is inevitable! You can also, count on that you can never go back to *the way we were*. The change came in a big way for me. The marriage broke up, the job disappeared, the horse got sick (sounds like the perfect Country Western song), and I left Dallas for the small-town life of Austin, Texas.

During this time, events overpowered me mentally, and one thing led to another until I was not even able to earn a living. Still, I had two kids to care for, trying to keep a roof over our heads and food on the table.

It was about two weeks before Christmas. I had managed to get a scant few presents for the kids, which I had hidden in the trunk of the Lincoln. I fell behind on my payments. What happened next was obvious. One morning the car was gone! I didn't even think of repossession, so I called the police. They told me to contact the bank. Of course, the bank repossessed the car, but It was still in Austin.

The tow truck guy told me where to go for the personal effects out of the car, which I did. Small comfort that Christmas would not be a complete disappointment for the kids.

I had no idea what to do next, but I had to have a car. A good friend in Dallas said he had an old VW that had rolled over but still ran. Would I like to use it until I got on my feet? Man, that was like music to my ears. I booked a cheap, one way, Southwest Airlines flight to Dallas to get the VW. What happened next is the title of another chapter. *"Listen to the Teacher Within."*

Intuition is a derivative of a Latin word (*intueri*) meaning 'teacher from within or the ability to know something without having proof.'

The morning I was to fly to Dallas. I noticed an extra set of car keys on the dresser. The *'teacher'* said to me in a loud and clear voice (mine, I think) "take the keys, or you will always have regrets." I had no reason to pick up the keys. The car was gone!

Still, I grabbed the keys.

My friend picked me up at the airport when I got to Dallas. On the drive back to his house, beyond belief, was my beloved Lincoln Continental in the bank's parking lot. Well, as you can imagine, my heart pounded and my face flushed. I knew why 'the voice' told me to take the keys. Without a moment's hesitation, I asked him to take me around the block and back to 'my' car. With the swiftness of a car thief, I opened the door and started the car. I drove the Lincoln off the lot to his garage to hide the Lincoln for the night. It was Sunday, so I knew no one would miss it until Monday morning.

It was later, at the friend's house, that I made my plan. I would get up at four o'clock on Monday morning drive to Austin and put the car in a storage shed. I never gave a thought to *where* I would store the car, or even if there was a storage bin large enough or available. That Monday morning began the adventure destined to change my life.

My plan is working. The drive takes about three and a half hours. A little after 7:00 AM, I arrived at a nearby storage facility, and incredibly, one was available. With the car safely in storage, I walked home.

Sure enough! On Monday I got a call from the bank, fishing for information about the car. I am sure they suspected I had it, but could not find it, nor prove I taken the Lincoln. Wow! Exciting stuff, but at least I had my beautiful Lincoln back. It was that important to me. The car represented '*me*' as a successful man. Having it repossessed was not an option.

Somehow, I bought a rundown old vehicle. The driver's side window did not 'roll' up, and the windshield wipers did not work at all.

Months went by while I drove the old car to try to get back in the groove. Occasionally on a Sunday, I would go to the storage shed to get the Lincoln and take the kids for a ride in the country to touch base with what once was the reality.

A friend living in New Orleans knew of my plight. She called one day and said, "You can't drive that car in Texas, bring it to New Orleans, where it's not hot." "You can use my car until you get back on your feet." I know I cried.

Off to New Orleans to get her car. Returning to

Austin with very little money in my pocket, just breathing room,

Her selfless act encouraged me to get back on track.

I knew of a man who ran a direct sales company, and although I didn't like him or the product, I asked for a job. I knew that I could make some serious money quickly, but I was desperate. The first week I earned $90.00! More money than I had seen in one place in a long time.

Within a few months, I was making four or five hundred dollars a week. Nine months after *'stealing'* my car, I flew to Dallas with a pocket full of cash, walked into the bank and asked to speak to the President of the bank. It was in his office that I told him I wanted to pay off the loan.

He informed me that the car had disappeared and that the insurance company paid the bank. I asked him to get the insurance representative on the phone to find out how much the claim had been. He told me $2200.00. I put twenty-two, hundred-dollar bills on his desk, told him I had the Lincoln, and now I wanted the title! I'll never forget that look on his face. I am pretty sure he never forgot me. There was never a time that I thought I was committing a crime. It was my car; it had always been my car.

Next, I called New Orleans and told her what just happened; I am coming to get my car.

As you can imagine the ride back to Austin was one of triumph. I was very proud of myself.

I saved the airline ticket, the keys to the car, the

contract, even the parking receipt at the airport. To this day, I have a wooden collage on the wall with the words "NEVER GIVE UP!" I never gave up on that car, and I never gave up on myself!

How can you go wrong? Defeat lies in *giving up; you* have no chance to accomplish your goals. If you hang in there, you also have no choice. You **will** succeed. The more difficult road is to stick with your mission.

If you give up and go along another path, don't you have to start all over? Which way is easier? Starting over or staying with that with which you are already familiar?

On one of the Apollo missions, the command center, when faced with a problematic situation said, "failure is not an option." Make it your life's buzzword.

When hope is lost, the end comes quickly. Remember, *never, never give up!*

2

NEVER WORRY ABOUT THINGS OVER WHICH YOU HAVE NO CONTROL

Many people worry needlessly about:

• The weather. *Can your worry change this?*

• The neighbors. *How can your worry change this?* It's none of your business.

• Things left to chance. *Worry can't change this!* Chance is a gamble at best.

• What is everyone else doing? *How can your worry change this?* You can follow, or you can lead, your choice.

• What might happen in the future? The future is, at best, a vision in your imagination.

• Things from the past. *How can your worry change this?* It's too late to worry now!

Just don't worry about things over which you have no control. Worry and concern are two different things. It is smart to be concerned about the things you *can* change. It is utterly ridiculous to worry about the things you can't change!

Worry changes nothing so why waste functional mind space?' You cannot live in a *forgotten past nor the imagined future*. You can only live in the *clear and present now*! Enjoy 'the now,' and you'll have a better opportunity to succeed in the future. The future follows all of today's actions. Today, you are <u>*a product of yesterday's thought.*</u> This concept is vital for you to understand.

If stress, worry, and other harmful wastes of *'mind space'* consumes you today there is no chance to build for a happy and prosperous tomorrow. If yesterday's thought was full of worry, what would you expect life to be like for you today?

Effective thought processes do not include worry. They include planning, caring, and paying attention to the cause and effect in the world about you. Cause and effect apply to everything we do. The worry today brings no solution tomorrow.

There's a stream of trouble across my path;

It is dark and deep and wide.

Bitter the hour the future hath,

When I cross its swelling tide.

But I smile and sing and say:

"I will hope and trust always;

I'll bear the sorrow that comes tomorrow,

But I'll borrow none today."

Tomorrow's bridge is a dangerous thing;

I dare not cross it now.

I can see its timbers sway and swing,

And its arches reel and bow.

O heart, you must hope always;

You must sign and trust and say;

"I'll hear the sorrow that comes tomorrow,

But I'll borrow none today."

Hannah Whitall Smith

The Serenity Prayer sums this up very well!
"God grant me the serenity to accept the things
I cannot change; courage to change the things I
can; and the wisdom to know the difference."

Reinhold Niebuhr

3

EVERYTHING HAPPENS FOR YOUR OWN GOOD

———∽∽———

You may find this chapter challenging to believe. You probably will have to go deep into the memory of your life's experiences to find a reason for belief in this rule. Here is the one place that retrospect (hindsight) has great value. It is easier to see where in one's past an event, thought to be catastrophic, turned out for the betterment of all concerned.

Each of us has had these kinds of experiences. The critical thing to remember is to have faith, when confronted with adversity, to know that all will turn out for your greater good. If you take a good look at what it means to have faith, (*a firm belief in something for which there is no proof*) you might conclude that circumstances might just as well happen for your greater good. Thinking otherwise leads to damaging negative thoughts.

I remember once as a young man; I met an interesting woman during a sales call. I was selling carpet in Chicago for one of the area's largest firms. Since I was the youngest and newest of the sales force, I got the worst leads (sales calls). One day a sales call came into the office to meet a woman just a few blocks from our store. I thought it strange that I got the lead. I usually had to drive forty or fifty miles to get to the customer's home. When I got to the house, it was in incredible disarray, periodicals, newspaper, and books stacked in every corner. This woman was in no way ready to move all that clutter and put down new carpet.

We talked for only a few minutes about decorating her home, but as we spoke, the subject turned to things metaphysical. I'm not even sure of how or why we got into that conversation. At least I didn't know then. I think I now know. She had great insight and told me many things about myself that she couldn't have known, I had only just met this woman. She knew I had marital issues and told me she saw impending knee problems that would develop much later. What stuck with me was her lesson for that day, which, was " **When the student is ready, the teacher will appear."**

Now that was powerful stuff for me to remember for over fifty years. It was correct then, and it still is today. Our role in life is that of *student* and *teacher*. We may meet people for only a brief moment in their lives, possibly leave an impression for a lifetime. Look at every situation as an opportunity to enrich someone else's life, enhancing your own experience in return.

4

LISTEN TO THE TEACHER WITHIN

———∼∼∼———

Intuition has been a great *mother of learning* for all of human history. Some have learned to listen to their intuition. Many have gone on to be inventors, business leaders, or even the greatest prophets of all time. Women naturally listen to their intuition, possibly because women have the responsibility of childbearing and motherhood. Very creative people also listen carefully to *that little inner voice*. Do you hear your *inner voice?*

When I was a kid, the Catholic Church used to refer to the little voice as our *conscience*. Nearly every day we heard, '*Let your conscience be your guide.*' We knew right from wrong even if we didn't always pay attention to the message. When we heard that little voice say 'NO,' we knew what was wrong but, often did it anyway. Where does it lead? Trouble! Always leads to trouble!

Another story comes to mind. I was about twelve or thirteen years old. We had only the alleys in which to play with the kids in the neighborhood. Our neighborhood was in the path of the Cook

County Medical Center construction. That meant lots of buildings were being demolished all around us. Destruction and rubble went on as long as I can remember as a child.

There was an old man in the neighborhood we knew as 'Mr. Proctor.' We just called him, *Proctor*. He was, indeed, the all-time best scavenger and collector of neat things.

We often called on *Proctor* to supply us with nails, hinges or wood to build our *clubhouses* in the backyards, under stairways and in the empty lots of the area.

I must have needed just some such treasure, and I knew where to get it. Off I went to Proctor's backyard. Going through the gate, I saw what looked like red velvet bags in a garbage can. The voice inside me said, "these bags are important!" Investigate! I asked Proctor, "what's in them?" "I don't know," came the reply. Being a curious kid, I asked permission to look inside.

What I saw was a shock! There, lying on the red velvet was the glitter of gold. Bright, beautiful, precious gold!

These were the vestments of The Holy Catholic Church. I recognized them, because like almost all Catholic schoolboys, I had been an altar boy.

Closer inspection revealed the name of the church, *Blessed Sacrament Parish*. My inner voice told me what to do next. I must report this to the police. Proctor, by the way, had nothing to do with this. He picked up anything that might have value.

The police returned the *vestments* to the church.

It was just a day or two later that I got a message from Monsignor O'Brien, the parish pastor. Monsignor O'Brien asked me to come to his office where he gave me a book entitled *Nice Going Red*, which he had written. A story about actions by a troubled young boy. I still have the book.

I was heralded as a young hero for finding these sacred items and rewarded with my first-year tuition paid at St. Phillip High School.

My intuition had paid off. I listened to the voice directing me to the red velvet bags and what they meant to the church.

This small story has remained with me all these

years understanding the importance of listening, then acting upon the little voice within.

I bet that if we all sat around and compared stories, we could write another book about our experiences. The critical thing is to act on what your intuition tells you is the right thing to do.

Intuition is a noun whose definition means that someone has a quick understanding to interpret but without using reasoning. The word comes from the Latin roots in meaning *at or on* and *tueri (true)* meaning *to watch over.*

It's an automatic, effortless feeling that often quickly motivates us to act. Saving pain and sorrow or leading to great rewards.

5

AN IDLE MIND
IS THE DEVIL'S
WORKSHOP

————✧————

Visualize your mind as a kind of container. For the sake of this conversation, the *container* holds pure positive thought, a happy and productive mind.

We are also continually bombarded with influences both from outside our mind-space and our negative thoughts. We may not have any control over the attacks from the exterior, but how we deal with them affects what influence they have on our lives. But first, we must understand the danger of our negative *junk thinking* that can corrupt the peaceful, pure positive mind space.

Let's look at how this works. High school physics tells us that *'no two objects can occupy the same space, at the same time.' The Pauli Exclusion Principal*

Ralph Waldo Emerson [May 25, 1803 – April 27, 1882]

American philosopher and poet said: *"Thoughts are things."*

The following graphic gives us a simple visual of how thought affects us. In this example, if thoughts are things, then every *idea* created in your mind occupies its own actual space.

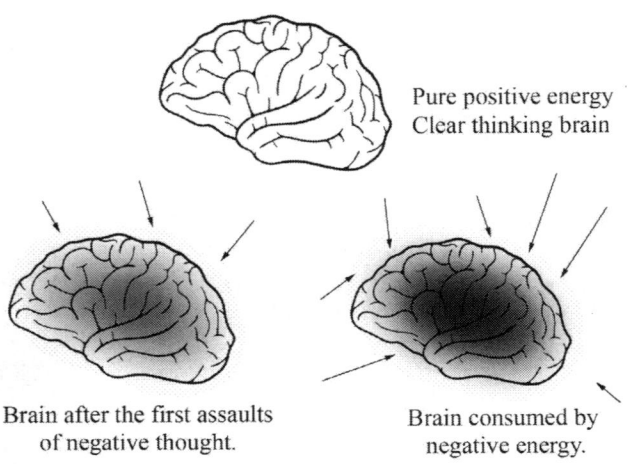

Pure positive energy
Clear thinking brain

Brain after the first assaults
of negative thought.

Brain consumed by
negative energy.

This graphic is an illustration of the human brain in various stages of negative attacks.

These 'thought things' occupy space and time in your mind. We will treat both the internal and external attacks in the same way, since both are damaging to the positive mind space.

The illustrations above give you an idea of what

happens when you allow even the first attack of negative thought (represented by the arrows) to penetrate the perfect bright (positive) mind space.

In the first illustration, you are 'sailing' along in a perfect world of positive energy. The power of positive energy can resist any attack from a negative source.

In the second illustration, the mind-space has allowed some harmful energy penetration, believing that it is strong enough to resist the attack.

The third illustration shows the result of allowing even the first attack to penetrate. Result, totally negative mind space! Negative energy and negative thoughts are going in all directions in and out of the mind-space.

Here in the illustration, the power of the mind has been turned over to the elements we do not desire, possibly totally out of control. What do you think this negative mind will attract? You are correct if you said *negative energy*. In this state, it is challenging to force the negative (black) thoughts out so that, pure (white) positive thinking can live within.

The use of the words black and white is used to refer to contrasting illustrations.

Each little negative thought you let into the pure, positive mind-space will push out positive thinking. Remember that the physical properties of *thought* will not allow two ideas to occupy the same space in your mind at the same moment. Since there cannot be space in this mind container, negative thinking allowed to enter will result in a positive thought (space) being forced to leave.

Once the negative thought enters, weakening the positive mind-space, it becomes easier for the next negative thought to invade this precious positive space.

The healthy, positive mental state is the time to be the most cautious and aware of negative thoughts. It is far too easy to think that we can afford even one little negative thought to invade. These negative thoughts can come in the form of a breach against the Cardinal Virtues or even your values. The smallest negative thinking will dilute the pure, positive mind space. You think it won't hurt to entertain a negative idea since in a positive energy state you feel so strong.

Not so! In the end, one thought leads to another until you have corrupted all the positive energy 'space' in your mind.

When enough negative thought penetrates the protective barrier of positive energy, the scales tip to predominately negative, now you are faced with the job to chase out the bad (negative) energy, replacing with the positive thought-space. For some, this difficulty can lead to depression, and all that comes along with being depressed.

Keeping one thought from entering is far more manageable than changing the whole makeup of the mind. That's why we must be ever vigilant to that first negative thought and not let it penetrate. Stop it at the gate of your mind to preserve the positive energy inside.

The way to control this process is simple. Just say 'NO.' When the temptation comes along, say 'NO.' First, you must learn to recognize the danger. I'll create some examples of the smallest of these negative thoughts, for which you must watch.

• Man, what lousy weather
• A guy cuts you off in traffic
• A waiter is slow or inattentive
• You get a flat tire

You get the idea! Little things that we can all experience in everyday life. If you allow the luxury of these little negative thoughts to enter your mind, dwelling upon them, they will, eventually, replace the positive, productive energy that once lived there.

When you weaken this space, you leave yourself open for more of the same to follow. Remember the rule that *'like attracts like?'* When the mind space is positive, it attracts positive energy. If the mind space is negative, it attracts negative energy. Just as simple as that! See where I am going with this?

How to change all this? Well, that's the remarkable part. All you have to do is **"Change Your Vocabulary."**

• It's raining, but we need the rain
• I think I'll slow down and let that driver in
• The waiter is busy cut him some slack

• Good thing the tire is flat now possible, preventing more problems later.

Now, do you get the message? It's not what happens **to you**, but how **you perceive** what is happening. That is what this book is all about. Redefine the thoughts, words, and events in your life. It will work miracles for you and, you don't have to do anything but *change the words you use.*

Refer to the chapter about the *'screen of your mind.'* Apply these principals here, and you'll see them work immediately.

Don't let your mind wander into the abyss of negative thinking and don't let your mind lie idle. A negative thought can fly into the open space of a vacant or wandering mind. Keep it focused on the right, wholesome, and the positive things you would like to have in your life.

A helpful hint would be to watch for words with a negative connotation like *can't, won't or* any phrase that brings a negative thought to mind. This behavior is very destructive. Change *can't* to; I **can.** Change *won't* to; I **will.**

So easy and yet so effective. Try it today!

6

WE ARE RULED BY OUR WEAKNESS

———————

In case you have forgotten (or never knew) these are the seven deadly sins and the seven cardinal virtues.

SINS	VIRTUES
Envy	Love
Lust	Faith
Greed	Hope
Sloth	Fortitude
Anger	Justice
Pride	Temperance
Gluttony	Prudence

If I left this page blank sooner or later, you might understand just what rule number six means.

Does greed drive you? That is a weakness. If gambling drives you, that is also a weakness. Does lust drive you? That too is a weakness. Each of these is among the sins against the cardinal virtues.

Time devoted to any of them is time taken away from constructive, positive energy. The kind of energy that provides the life you want.

What's on your mind most of the time? Do you spend more time with *sin* than you do with *virtue?*‘ None among us is perfect, but using the table above decide for yourself where you spend your *mind space*!

"You fence your yard!" What do you suppose I mean by this sentence?

A fence is designed to define the perimeter of your property. To keep others out and to limit what development occurs within. Your mind works the same way. Select and set the boundary. You build the fence that limits the growth of your life.

If you are not happy with the present conditions, consider moving *the fence!*

It is said, *'on the ladder of success, you can only climb as high as the ladder you choose to carry.'*

The taller ladder is much more difficult to carry, but the rewards are much higher.

The ladder and fence examples are another way of illustrating how we might limit our success and happiness in our own lives.

If weakness defines your perimeter weakness is what you get.

Tear down the old fence and grab the biggest ladder you can find. You'll be happy that you did!

7

SURRENDER YOUR PROBLEMS TO THE HIGHER POWER

———— ∾ ————

This one ought to be evident to the reader, but often overlooked.

Remember, this is a book based on faith, and as such, rule number seven requires trust in God.

Many of life's difficulties cannot be dealt with by the mortal power of man alone. These times are better given up to the Higher Power.

I learned a phrase along the way, and so I use it in teaching situations. It goes like this, *"The God of your understanding,"* which I later learned the phrase comes from the Twelve Steps of Recovery.

If you can surrender your problems to '*The God of your understanding*,' think of the relief you will experience by knowing that you have done all you can and left the rest to the Greatest Power ever!

Now wait, don't get me wrong here. Don't expect that you don't have to do a thing! That's not quite how it works, however. You must give one hundred percent of your effort to your life one hundred percent of the time. When conditions are overpowering and beyond your control, turn them over to and trust God.

You are no longer responsible for trying to change things over which you have no control.

An example of this comes to mind is one of my own experiences.

Four of us were in a small single-engine Cessna aircraft, flying from Milwaukee to Janesville, Wisconsin.

The purpose of the trip was to pick up papers for a registered Quarter Horse and to get nighttime hours for the young pilot. The control tower told us of the impending 'weather' expected at the

Milwaukee County Airport around nine o'clock that evening. We assumed we would be back long before nine, so that didn't appear to be an issue. We didn't even consider what was to happen. Fog and heavy cloud cover were what the control tower meant by the 'weather.'

The flight was beautiful, so we thought, *as long as we are in the area,* we would fly into the Playboy Club in Lake Geneva. Wow! That was a great experience. Staff members met us on the runway with a golf cart, and we got the red-carpet treatment in the Club. We knew we didn't have much time to enjoy our visit, so we left in about an hour.

The Club had a private airstrip. There was no tower, only a windsock. We took off and at less than 500 feet found ourselves in a thick, dense fog.

We were airborne, so there was no way to *go around* to land. There were zero visibility conditions, so we climbed to a few thousand feet, hoping to get above the fog. It just didn't happen. I remember the eerie feeling of knowing I was airborne but had no sense of direction, altitude, or speed.

Milwaukee County Airport radioed information that the fog covered two hundred square miles, the airport closed to all but instrument-rated pilots. Of course, my young friend had no such experience. Even though he could probably have been 'talked' down by the tower, he didn't want to lose the license he had worked so hard to attain, so we asked for directives instead. The tower told us that Janesville was the last reported area of patchy cloud cover. We set a compass heading back to Janesville.

We flew blind for about forty-five minutes during which time there was no panic in the aircraft. Compass headings can be accurate, but a light plane is subject to crosswinds that cause the aircraft to 'crab,' possibly blowing the compass heading off by a hundred miles. We knew we had to come down sooner or later, but I still couldn't see beyond the windshield.

It became my job to watch the altimeter, fuel gauges, and horizontal indicator. The pilot kept an eye on the compass, calculated distance and wind direction.

Miraculously, I spotted a small opening in the

cloud cover. Seeing what looked like a blinking light, I asked the pilot, *"is that an airport?"* He said he thought it was, so we headed down through the small opening in the dense fog. The first landing attempt was almost the end. The weather reports we had received were about an hour old, so the wind direction was not accurate. We attempted landing in a crosswind. As soon as one wheel touched the ground, the plane dipped a wing towards the runway. The pilot's quick action powering up to go around saved four lives that night, mine included. After two landing attempts, we were finally on the ground. Safe and sound, I jumped out of the aircraft, dropped to my knees, and kissed the ground.

We all knew we would make it. The faith in the

Higher Power was on our side. I now know the meaning of "God is my co-pilot."

It's great to have God on your team; you are the coach, so 'send him in.'

8

GIVE YOURSELF THE SAME SLACK YOU GIVE EVERYONE ELSE

Teachers in the Catholic school system used to

grade by the number system. I suppose some teachers still do the same today.

A passing grade was 70, and at the very least, that was the goal.

If you got a 69 on your report card, you failed the course. You likely have to make the course up in summer school.

Think about what that means; you only had to be right seven out of ten times. Something like our present-day weather forecasters.

Another example would be professional sports, baseball, for instance. If a batter who hits 300 or better, is considered a great hitter. Holy Cow! That means only three out of ten times he gets on base and he is <u>successful</u>?

If a baseball team wins half the games, they are

said to be at *five hundred*. They are considered
<u>successful</u>. See where I am going with all this?

We admire others who are successful as little as
<u>one out of three times</u>, yet we expect much more
of ourselves. We may even expect perfection!
Isn't that ridiculous? We hold ourselves to a
higher standard than the most celebrated
baseball hitters of all time. Expecting perfection
is setting yourself up for disappointment or even
failure.

You should cut yourself some slack. Allow for
error, and you will reduce your stress level
immensely. Reducing stress increases the chance
of success. You don't expect others to be perfect.
No one ever heard of a batter hitting 1000, or a
team winning all of their games. (Although, the
Miami Dolphins did it once.)

In the game of life, seventy is passing, and nobody is perfect.

Remember, failure is just what happens to people who don't succeed, so you have one of two choices. Either you win or lose! There isn't any middle ground.

Winning is not necessarily always immediate. Winning consists of several small steps all put together toward the ultimate goal.

There is an old expression that says, "I may have lost the battle, but I didn't lose the war."

Success is not measured by suddenly being there!

I don't believe that you are ever successful.

I think that you are always on the road to being successful.

GIVE YOURSELF THE SAME SLACK YOU GIVE EVERYONE ELSE

9

BE NICE TO THE PEOPLE

Just be 'nice' to everyone you meet or come in contact with every day. What could be more simple than that?

"Do unto others as you would have them do unto you!"

Be kind to the people, and you will be treated kindly in return. Simple, isn't it? I learned this expression when I was twenty-one, back in Chicago. Being an outside salesman, I would go into the main office quite often. *George* was the office manager and motivator of salespeople.

I'll never forget *George* from those days. He was a rather rotund man with a deep voice. Every time I went into the office, he could be heard admonishing everyone to "Be 'nice' to the people," almost growling.

It became a motto I try to live by every day. Remember the Golden Rule of 'doing unto others!'

Make it a point to bring a smile to a stranger's face as you go through your day.

10

THE SCREEN OF YOUR MIND

How *Mind Space* works and why positive input is so valuable is *the* essential value received from reading this book. You must read, re-read, and read again until you understand this concept! This concept is not *'rocket science'* but once understood; it will change your life forever.

The mind consists of three distinct parts.

The conscious mind (what we see and hear daily)

The unconscious mind (deep mind)

The Universal Mind (God Mind)

I call the unconscious mind *'The Deep Mind,'* and for the sake of this writing will refer to it as such.

The conscious or aware mind directs the Deep Mind, that which you see and hear daily. All thoughts and visions in your conscious mind are directives to the Deep Mind, always acting for your highest good.

The Deep Mind operates in the realm of the

Universal Mind (The God-Mind) bringing about your highest good for you.

The Universal Mind, acting upon that which the deep mind directs, by way of your visions and deeply held desires. The Universal Mind is your gateway to all knowledge and power. The connection between the conscious and the deep mind accounts for the ability to tap into the power of the Universe.

I refer to this connection as 'the screen of your mind.' Here is where visions begin. Once seen clearly and believed, these visions are more easily manifested by 'The God of Your Understanding.'

Does this sound a bit metaphysical? It does because it is! The Universal Mind is that part of us, which is the eternal, all-knowing, Infinite God.

I believe that we all share in this 'God-Mind.' In this state all things are possible, and everything can come to you.

Think of it as being in harmony with the Great Architect of the Universe, The Holy Spirit, God!

The deep mind being in contact with the God Mind is an all-powerful, all-knowing entity. Nothing is beyond the power of this connection. Learn to trust it, and many of your everyday difficulties will fade into obscurity.

JUST THREE CONDITIONS ARE NEEDED TO IMPLEMENT THIS CONNECTION.

You MUST *clearly*, <u>see on</u> the screen of your mind, that which you desire. Visualizing can be aided by images seen in magazines, by drawings you do, or by that which you see in the world about you. *Seeing* is the key!

You MUST <u>*believe*</u> you are worthy of your vision. Here is where your faith comes into play. The knowledge that your 'God' has the power to bring what you request. The genuine need of your entire being. That your vision is loving and a well thought through decision.

You MUST begin to _act as_ if your vision is already a reality. An action is an act of faith bolstered by understanding steps one and two above. All three of these requirements *MUST* present if you expect a successful, positive outcome.

REMEMBER
ALWAYS! SEE-BELIEVE-ACT!

Life doesn't just become the proverbial "bowl of cherries." It's just not like that. Problems are part of life and given to us as tests. Obstacles provide an opportunity, with which, to harmonize with the Universal Mind.

See a further explanation in the next chapter.

Part II

'Three simple steps to manifest whatever you desire.'

THOUGHTS ALONG THE WAY

11

THREE SIMPLE STEPS TO MANIFEST WHATEVER YOU DESIRE

SEE – BELIEVE – ACT!

1. **See** a clear image of that which you

desire (demand) on the *screen of your mind!*

2. **Believe** with all your being that you deserve the image you have created.

3. **Act** as if you have already attained your desire.

Step One can be as simple as putting a note on your bathroom mirror. See it every day! It can be an affirmation like 'I am well' or 'I am strong.' It can even be a clipping from a magazine or a picture downloaded from an online source. A car, a house, even a new romance, anything you strongly desire. The image must be realistic and exact, not just wishful thinking.

Step Two, you must confirm your desire. Believe it without reservation. You are an extension of 'The Creator!' That energy will bring your picture into focus and then reality. The critical point here is not to doubt or worry about how this will happen. Give it up to the 'God Within.' 'The God of Your Understanding' then go about your business knowing that it <u>is your birthright</u>. Yes, you are born to be an extension of Creation. This affirmation is part of the *ongoing Creation*.

Step Three instructs you to relax and trust in God. Continue to work every day on steps one and two. If you do, you will soon realize that which you have set in motion. When you do come to that realization, you may even laugh out loud astounded as to how it happened and how fast! Seemingly by magic!

STOP READING RIGHT HERE! Don't read another thing until you have reread this chapter and you understand what you have learned.

I have an affirmation taped to my cabinet above my desk.

"Good Morning, Bill!"

"This is God."

"I will be handling all of your problems today."

"I will not need your help, so have a miraculous day!"

12

OUR SOCIETY
AS A PYRAMID

Visualize a pyramid in your mind, see it clearly with all the steps and layers of blocks. The pyramid shape is comparable to our society's structure. The base of the monument has a broad, expansive footing. See it in your mind's eye, gradually work your way up the sides of the pyramid, to the very top. We find the pinnacle, where only one stone is in place, reigning over the stones below. All of the blocks at the base of the pyramid support the entire weight. The last course, at the top, holds nothing above. Notice that each of the blocks is similar in size with the first course being more populated with stone. Each layer rising to the pinnacle has less stone, therefore carrying less weight.

The comparison of how our society is structured begins with the laborer, commonly referred to as the 'working class.' Some of which are the builders of our world, the grassroots of our society who also form the largest numbers and do the most significant amount of physical work. They build a structure that supports all the weight.

The higher up the pyramid we travel, we see fewer people with the rarest at the very top. This vast difference from the most substantial numbers to the fewest is in a direct comparison between the 'builders' and the elite few who are, generally, the wealthiest and the managers of all the layers below.

Between pinnacle and base are the majority, consisting of middle management, small to medium-sized businesses and professional people.

Understand the functions of these layers, beginning with the builders, the keepers of the whetstone of our society.

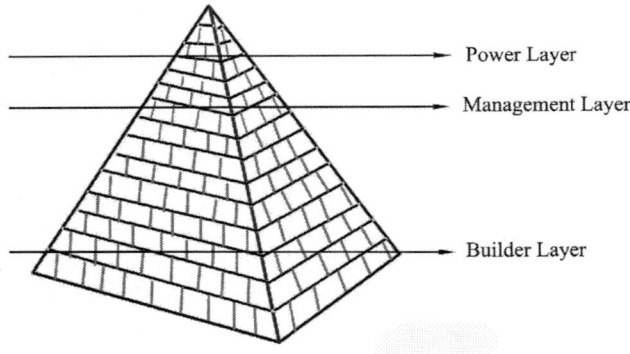

In the middle is the conductor, the mover of all effort, material, and wealth of the building class. The responsibility of the center is to distribute the 'fruit of the labor' of the builders to the many layers above and below the middle. The middle class is the 'transfer' agent of all wealth, products, and commerce.

The power connection is at the top. The leaders, political, economic, educational, and spiritual, in this way, the pinnacle is responsible for all the layers below. Money, for instance, serves no purpose remaining exclusively at the top. For the social function to survive, the resources must move and flow from one level to the other, back and forth, thereby keeping the whole society fluid.

Everyone in the social scheme is protective of their product, labor, and more especially, the rewards of their effort. We hear those in the base of the structure wanting more money and often envious or angry at those who, seeming, have it all at the top.

This struggle has been constant since human beings began polishing stones, that was carried in a small pouch to trade with others who also polished stones. Some were larger or prettier than others, and so the barter or exchange of goods and services began.

Can you imagine turning the pyramid upside down? With the few that were at the pinnacle now at the bottom, with the weight of all the people and (stones) crashing down and crushing them. Total collapse for the ancient pyramids of the planet and the social structure experienced in our society.

It is necessary to have many types of people at many different levels of abilities even though we don't prefer to view ourselves as a classist society.

What separates us from other social structures such as, feudal, dictatorship, or monarchies is that we can move up the stepping stones of the pyramid.

The ancient structures were not built with smooth sides. Instead, blocks assembled as stepping stones with plaster filling the spaces between the rock. In this way, the builders could continue moving materials to the pinnacle of the structure.

In the same way, it suffices to say that any of us can climb the social stepping stones to a higher place. Only the restrictions by the individual, their strengths, desires, and needs to determine where they fit in the social structure.

I am using this analogy to reach, beyond what you see around you.

Feast your eyes on the next level! It is possible, and it is attainable!

CHANGE YOUR VOCABULARY

13

BE CAREFUL
WHAT YOU
WISH FOR

You are a product of yesterday's thought! Your thinking of yesterday programmed your reality of today. In the same way, what you are thinking about right now will direct tomorrow's reality.

Look at your life now, and decide is this what you want for the future?

You have a choice. Remembering what you read here will prepare you to put into practice the change you desire in a real way.

Little things like how you answer everyday greetings. "How are you doing?" Pay attention to how you answer the question. Many times, you will hear, "Oh, I guess I'll make it!" or just "OK." What does it say? I believe that a person is setting themselves for *just making it tomorrow* or just being 'OK' for tomorrow or maybe *for a lifetime.*

Often I hear..."Oh, I am OK for now," at which point I feel compelled to ask ..." for now, why?"

"Are you expecting something bad to happen soon?"

I would rather hear people speak words like these, *"terrific, fantastic, or I am doing well,"* followed up with "How about yourself ?" Two things will happen if you make a habit of answering with an enthusiastic, positive affirmation.

1. You will be training all your tomorrows to be just as you directed, fantastic, terrific, etc.!

2. You will leave many people wondering why life is terrific and wonderful for you and not for them. Should they ask, give them a little bit of *Change Your Vocabulary?*

Another little story. A few years ago, I stopped

in a convenience store to purchase gas for my vehicle. A young man came in, apparently known to the counter clerk who asked, in the casual way most of us do, "How's it going?"

After that, the customer said: Oh, I gotta go to work today!"

I must tell you that I wouldn't mind my own business and said something like this "you *gotta* go to work today?" "Aren't you the least bit happy that you have a job?" I hope he thought about that later.

Listen to the way people chart their futures with their vocabulary.

14

THE CREATIVE FORCE THAT BINDS US

I often find myself in a crowded room with the ear of someone that wants to hear what I have to say. I will ask that person a simple question, which I now ask of you.

What does everyone in this room have in common? For that matter, what does everyone in this country have in common? Moreover, what does everyone in the world who has ever lived or ever will live have in common? As you might expect, the answers range from the need to be loved, the normal bodily functions, and that we will all die? While all of these and other responses are true, the answer I am looking for is, **our body temperature!**

In physics, a law of thermodynamics, also known as the Law of Conservation of **Energy**, states that energy can neither be created nor destroyed. Energy can only be transferred or changed from one form to another.

Our body temperature is a form of energy. There may be lots of medical theories as to what creates this energy. Further examination fails to identify the *source* of energy. Theories of creating nothing from nothing abound, and one can get lost in quantum physics. For this exercise, we say, all living creatures share in this energy of life.

The very essence that keeps humans on or about 98.6 *is* The Creative Force. The 'Life Force' that lives within us *is* the Energy of Creation. In that way, we are all *one* in the continuing creation. We are all brothers and sisters with the Oneness of the Universe. I mentioned earlier that the philosophy in this book revolves around faith in God the Creator.

What happens to the energy, that is the Creative Force, at the end of life?

Is it reasonable to believe that through a process

similar to osmosis, defined as the movement of a liquid passing through a semi-permeable membrane into a solution of a higher concentration, which tends to equalize the concentrations of solute on both sides of the membrane?

A simple way to illustrate the process would be what happens when we sit in a bathtub for too long. The body loses fluid and skin wrinkles.

Since body heat is a form of energy which cannot be destroyed, even with the death of the physical body, what happens to the energy? It must, by physical law, dissipate into the larger energy field by osmosis, if you will.

I call the physical body 'The Tabernacle of our Intellect' or another way of expressing would be the *holding vessel* of our energy (soul).

The larger body of energy is the Creative Energy of all that was or ever will be. Upon death the vessel's contents are released from whence they came to be absorbed into the larger body — The Infinite Creative Force of The Universe.

None among us has ever experienced this energy exchange, but it is my hypothesis of what happens to the soul after death. For me, it is a logical explanation of what becomes of the creative energy within us all.

15

THE REED AND
THE WIND

⁓

Traveling around our beautiful country, you can
see tall grass plants swaying in the gentle breeze
of the spring wind. You can see these plants in
the waters of Florida or the plains of Kansas.
Anywhere I see these grasses I am reminded of
'The Reed and the Wind.'

Many go through life being the reed often swaying to the needs and wants, of others around them. Their life is left to chance, and the whim of desires outside themselves. Each of us has experienced being the 'reed,' but too few realize they can be the 'wind.'

By not bending in the slightest breeze of other's needs and wants, one becomes stronger to resist, sometimes adverse, outside circumstances.

There may be a hundred examples of being the 'reed,' and I bet you will find them in your own life. Someone or something changes your plans or direction, and you may bend to satisfy their needs instead of holding fast in your own need.

Those people who are more often the 'wind' are the most successful among us. 'Driven as the wind' means precisely that. See the destination, see the goal, letting little distract you.

Indeed, this does not mean *never change* your mind's direction. Be aware of <u>how</u> the *wind* is affecting your course.

With so many examples of life, teaching says that thinking of ourselves is selfish. Thinking about it, yes it is! However, there are times when selfish is the only path to survival. One of our fundamental needs is 'survival.' It's is part of our DNA. In that light, taking care of oneself and one's needs comes first. If you are not taking care of yourself, how can you take care of others?

You can't pour from an empty cup. There are times to take care of yourself first.

16

TURN OVER YOUR TENDERFOOT PIN EVERY DAY

———❧———

Growing up in the inner city of Chicago, one of my fondest memories was of the Boy Scouts of America. Looking back lessons they taught me then apply to daily life now.

Scout Law reminds me that "A Scout is Trustworthy, Loyal, Helpful, Friendly, Courteous, Kind, Obedient, Cheerful, Thrifty, Brave, Clean, and Reverent."

The Boy Scout Oath or Promise:

"On my honor, I will do my best. To do my duty to God and my country and to obey the Scout Law; To help other people at all times; To keep myself physically strong, mentally awake, and morally straight."

In addition to these practical lessons were the apparent skills of camping out, cooking, cleaning up after myself and tying knots, among other things. I often wondered why tying knots were going to be of value, but in the years since I've come to understand. The simple square knot needed to tie my shoelaces. Little things like these!

The first three levels of BSA rank were: Tenderfoot, Second Class, and First Class. Each of these levels required us to study and demonstrate proficiency to move on to another level. When we proved proficiency in the first level of Tenderfoot, we received the badge of the Tenderfoot. How proud I was to wear a Tenderfoot Pin! I still have that badge (pin) 65 years later, the very one you see pictured here.

Our Scout Master taught us, Tenderfoots, a neat trick to remind each of us of an essential part of the

Scout Oath. 'Help other people at all times!' We were required to wear the pin upside down every day until we did a good deed for someone during the day. It could be a stranger who we helped with groceries, even opening a door for a senior. Any little thing would get us the reward of turning our Tenderfoot Pin over.

The pin served to remind us of the oath, a powerful reminder of a duty.

Make a point of bringing a smile to someone's face every day. Everywhere you leave another person happy that you crossed their path.

Take this lesson with you. <u>Act like a Tenderfoot.</u> See what you can do every day to help make someone else's day better.

17

THINK ABOUT IT

~

"YOU CANNOT BEAT YOURSELF FOR

WHAT YOU DIDN'T DO...

BUT...

YOU CAN BEAT YOURSELF FOR

WHAT YOU DON'T DO!"

ABOUT CHANGE...

"ALL LIVING THINGS MUST

CONTINUE TO CHANGE OR THEY WILL

BEGIN TO DECAY.

THAT APPLIES TO PLANTS, HUMAN

BEINGS, OR A CITY."

"SOON THIS TIME,

WILL BE A LONG

TIME AGO."

IT IS THE PROHIBITION THAT MAKES ANYTHING PRICELESS

"DO RIGHT AND FEAR NOTHING!"

THE MISSION IN LIFE...

"LEARN EVERYTHING YOU CAN...

TEACH EVERYTHING YOU KNOW."

Have fun with your life and remember to
"Change Your Vocabulary."

Epilogue

Thoughts and ideas for 'Change Your Vocabulary,' the title and the concept started in 1975. In the ensuing years, life got in the way. The same sort of things that get into every life has kept me from finishing this book.

Some of the ideas in this book at one time or another were original. So much time has passed, it is now apparent that other authors have picked up on the same *Universal Knowledge* ideas, creating so many beautiful books.

For many of you, there will be nothing new in

this book but will serve as a reminder of what you already know.

For other's, there will be new and fresh ideas upon which to build.

My hope that this effort finds itself into the hearts of those who need new information most and to those who only need a reminder.

Special thanks to:

Carol Combs Photographer

creating the cover image.

APPENDIX

"Change Your Vocabulary" is an ongoing work and has been since the late '70s.

It is not now finished and may never be.

As an ongoing work, I will share with you what I learn,' *Along The Way*,'

Your Notes

YOUR THOUGHTS TO BE SHARED

Please feel free to send them along to the author.

info@changeyourvocabulary.com

QUESTIONS YOU MAY HAVE

Send questions to the author. I will attempt to get to as many as I can with an answer.

info@changeyourvocabulary.com

Made in the USA
Middletown, DE
04 July 2021